MW01712533

There Were Ten in the Bed

For my friend Linda
— S.C.C.

ISBN 0-439-72319-1

12 11 10 9 8 7 6 5 4 3 2 1 3 4 5 6 7 8/0
Printed in the U.S.A.
First Scholastic printing, September 2003

There Were Ten in the Bed

Illustrated by Susan Chapman Calitri

SCHOLASTIC INC.
New York Toronto London Auckland Sydney
Mexico City New Delhi Hong Kong Buenos Aires

There were ten in the bed
And the little one said,
"Roll over, roll over."

So they all rolled over
And one fell out.

There were nine in the bed
And the little one said,
"Roll over, roll over."

So they all rolled over
And one fell out.

There were eight in the bed
And the little one said,
"Roll over, roll over."

So they all rolled over
And one fell out.

There were seven in the bed
And the little one said,
"Roll over, roll over."

So they all rolled over
And one fell out.

There were six in the bed
And the little one said,
"Roll over, roll over."

So they all rolled over
And one fell out.

There were five in the bed
And the little one said,
"Roll over, roll over."

So they all rolled over
And one fell out.

There were four in the bed
And the little one said,
"Roll over, roll over."

So they all rolled over
And one fell out.

There were three in the bed
And the little one said,
"Roll over, roll over."

So they all rolled over
And one fell out.

There were two in the bed
And the little one said,
"Roll over, roll over."

So they all rolled over
And one fell out.

There was one in the bed
And the little one said,
"I FOUND IT!"

There Were Ten in the Bed

2. There were nine in the bed ...
(verses 3-9—count one less each repetition)

10. There was one in the bed and the
little one said, "I found it!"